Secrets of Making

I0060629

Title: Secrets of Making Money

ISBN-13: 978-0-9910285-9-7

Secrets of Making Money
teaches you the secrets of
bankers and rich investors. Learn
the secrets of making money and
change your life permanently.

Author: Kambiz Mostofizadeh

Publisher: Mikazuki Publishing
House

Secrets of Making Money

Introduction

When I was 21 years, I had 80 employees in 5 offices in 2 States. I have invested in various start-up companies and generated millions of dollars for others. Business, as I have learned over the past 26 years, is about trial and error. It is about practicality and doing what works. It is about perseverance in the face of difficulty. If you are able to absorb the difficulties of doing business, then you will be successful. Everyone is talented. Not everyone is dedicated. Not everyone is focused. This book will guide your business mindset and allow you to make business decisions with greater understanding. A good businessperson has many qualities including but not limited to, courage, honesty, high moral character, as well as a sixth sense like ability to have vision

Secrets of Making Money

about future events. The world is a history of business and monetary transactions. Every second, in every place on earth, money is being transacted. The world respects those with greater amounts of money but never takes the time to teach you how to become rich. There are no classes in any school that teach you how to get rich. There are no schools that teach you the secrets of making money. From a young age, we are taught not to think about money. Many believe that money is the root of all evil. Money is neither good nor bad, money is just money. Money is a medium of exchange for goods and services and that will be its only role as long as it exists. There is no formula for getting rich and certainly no one can predict the future, but there are rules to business and rules to money, which I share with you in this book.

Secrets of Making Money

LIFE LESSONS

What the hell is a life coach? Will they throw me a life preserver if I fail in business or in life? Here are 10 easy lessons for you.

1. Take every piece of disposable income you have and buy Gold with it.

2. Don't trust your money with anybody.

3. Get married earlier in life and have children earlier in life.

4. All politics is a waste of your time. Focus on your business and family.

5. Learn to produce things; Art. Books, Shoes, Software, Movies, etc.

Secrets of Making Money

6. Look for caring qualities in your future spouse rather than attractiveness.

7. Don't listen to anything anyone tells you, unless they are successful and have expertise in the subject at hand. No one can foretell the future or predict anything.

8. If you invest in a business that yields 18 percent a year return and if you re-invest that 18 percent a year for 20 years, $50,000 will become $2,000,000 from Compound Interest. Understand Compound Interest and it will make you rich.

9. Live frugal and beneath your means. The people that you want to impress hate you already so there

is really nothing to prove to anyone.

10. Help people when you can because you never know when you need someone else's help.

SWEAT EQUITY

To paraphrase Ray Kroc, the more you sweat the luckier you get. Businesses and empires are built by hard work and tireless dedication. The harder you work, the more opportunities will become available to you. No one in the history of business ever got rich by doing nothing. It took multiple steps to reach success and even then, success was not taken for granted. More work and greater productivity would be needed to maintain it. It is all about being dedicated enough to put aside any distractions and to just focus what has to be done.

Secrets of Making Money

Everyone has good and bad days. Everyone has days they may feel a bit gloomy. A champion is a person that can perform no matter what their mood is. You have to be able to teach your mind to put on blinders and to focus only on what has to be completed. Getting sidetracked is easy when there are screens everywhere and distractions all around you. You have to learn to tune out everything but your business and to create a business safe space where you can concentrate on your tasks without any distractions. It is important to have mental stamina when carrying out business tasks. You cannot lose patience or get tired easily. You have to have the mental stamina to continue carrying out your business tasks uninterrupted for long periods of time. You have to come to a simple understanding. Your

Secrets of Making Money

competitors have more people working more hours than you. That is why they are winning. You have to be more dedicated and put in more hours than your competitors in order to win. That means out-working them. Not an easy feat. A difficult feat but one that you will have to commit to if you want to win in business. The most dedicated, wins. That is the rule in business. If you are more dedicated and are willing to outwork your business competitors, then you may just be able to compete. The formula is known as TIMP.

Time – Businesses take time to grow. You cannot expect to achieve success overnight. It may take 5 years or 10 years or 20 years.

Information – You have to have real time business information so

Secrets of Making Money

that you can make informed
financial decisions.

Money – Money fuels labor,
logistics, retail space, etc. Money
fuels investments and drives
business.

People – You have to have
persons that can carry out tasks
that are related to operating your
business.

IT'S THE ECONOMY

The history of the United
States and Europe is littered with
the stories of entrepreneurs,
businessperson, and pioneers
that risked all to gain big. They
were essentially risk takers and
speculators that had the nerve
and courage to bear the minor or
major problems associated with
their ventures. Their level of
courage was higher than their

Secrets of Making Money

peers and their belief in themselves was superior to everyone around them. But in the end, they were just speculators that did prepare to meet success and they were very lucky indeed. Circumstances around you cannot be controlled. You can however meet the future with a plan reaching your success. Founder of the Hershey Corporation, Milton Hershey went bankrupt multiple times until he reached success with the sale of his caramel manufacturing unit allowing him to fund the building of Hershey, Pennsylvania. John Paul Getty experienced drilling many oil wells that yielded little or no oil before striking a gusher. The qualities that these men shared in common was their determination and persistence to push ahead in the face of clear

Secrets of Making Money

difficulties. There are situations
however that must be abandoned
depending on the investment at
hand, but for the most part it is
the determination and
persistence that pushes you
forward. Inventor Nikola Tesla
faced countless failures, battles
against other inventors that
attempted to claim Tesla's
inventions as their own, and
acute lack of funds. In spite of
this, Tesla was able to create the
world's most important
inventions. It was his
stubbornness and determination
that lead him to success, not his
skills. His skills allowed him to
create but his persistence and
determination lead him to the
finish line. That is the point of

why you are reading this book, to get to the finish line.

There will be more than a handful of people that will tell you what you want to do can't be done but that is really their inner voice telling you what they can't do. It is the projection of their fears unto you. They will tell you what not to do, but will never offer any solution as to what you should do. You should follow your own inner voice as to where you should invest your money.

 **Listen to your own investing voice.**

Secrets of Making Money

DO YOUR RESEARCH BEFORE

So many investors have been duped by fly-by-night companies that sold a miracle cure or a miracle solution. Snake oil salesmen were popular in Americana for their ability to sell anyone anything. They would convince you to buy a lotion or a bottle of liquid that contained some miracle cure or miracle solution to your problems. The lack of viable options many times sent the gullible, naïve, and bored masses to watch these snake oil salesmen hawking their wares. You can only be fooled if you are unaware of what is happening. You can only be fooled or convinced on a false premise if you did not do your research beforehand. Most of your time should be spent doing research and studying the lives of successful people. Most of your

Secrets of Making Money

time should be spent doing research on various business models. Most of your time should be spent learning about various companies, how they make money, and where they invest that money. There have been scores of hype selling modern snake oil salesmen that have duped venture capitalists and investors in to believing they have the miracle solution. To better understand the nature of humans when faced with the opportunity of riches, let us view this passage published in 1841 from author Charles Mackay.

"But the most absurd and preposterous of all, and which showed, more completely than any other, the utter madness of the people, was one started by an unknown adventurer, entitled 'A company for carrying on an undertaking of great advantage, but nobody to know what it is'.

14

Secrets of Making Money

Were not the fact stated by scores of credible witnesses, it would be impossible to believe that any person could have been duped by such a project. The man of genius who essayed this bold and successful inroad upon public credulity, merely stated in his prospectus that the required capital was 500,000 English Pounds Sterling, in five thousand shares of £100 each, deposit £2 per share. Each subscriber, paying his deposit, would be entitled to £100 per annum per share. How this immense profit was to be obtained, he did not condescend to inform them at that time, but promised, that in a month full particulars should be duly announced, and a call made for the remaining 98% of the subscription. Next morning, at nine o'clock, this great man opened an office in Cornhill. Crowds of people beset his door, and when he shut up at three

Secrets of Making Money

o'clock, he found that no less than one thousand shares had been subscribed for, and the deposits paid. He was thus, in five hours, the winner of £2,000 (worth over £2,000,000 in 2020). He was philosopher enough to be contented with his venture, and set off the same evening for the Continent. He was never heard of again."

- Charles Mackay, Memoirs of Extraordinary Popular Delusions (1841)

The above was presented to show that gullibility is a crime more of the greedy than it is of the un-knowledgeable. The people that bought shares in this company that feature a name that almost comedically and opening states that it had no set purpose other than a great undertaking. The white collar criminal that pulled this off played and banked on the greed of the masses and accordingly fled thereafter.

What I Learned From Getty

1. Getty believed that overhead costs are a lie and a scam, used only as cosmetic dressing to project an image of success. Getty signed all his oil contracts on the hood of his "Tin Lizzie" aka Model-T Ford. At the height of Getty's wealth, all his international oil ventures that generated tens of billions of dollars were run from a modest 5 story building that held no more than 100 people.

2. You cannot expect your employees to work harder than you. If you tell your employee to show up at 7:30am, you better be

there at 7am. Getty having himself worked as a roughneck on an oil rig, believed in leading from the front, not barking orders from the back.

3. Do not invest in a business that you cannot directly control. Better yet, the best business according to Getty is the business that you control, but own no stake in.

4. A sophisticated man is a man that loves art, theater, and music. Getty believed that the downfall of society (the creation of the un-sophisticated person) stems from its lack of appreciation for art.

5. Employees should be rewarded according to performance (bonuses)

and their annual salary
should be adjusted to
reflect the company's
strong or weak
performance.

What I Learned From Hershey

The frugal Dutchman went
bankrupt 7 times before
becoming a success but he never
gave up his determination to win.
His success wasn't Hershey
chocolate as that came after his
success with selling caramels for
a penny a piece. His success
with caramels funded Hershey
Chocolate Bars that were priced
at a nickel in the early 1900's. His
success from his caramels
funded the construction and
development of a rural township
in to a city called Hershey,
Pennsylvania. Before he was 60
years old, he gave away ALL his
riches to a Trust that still exists
today. This Trust created the

Secrets of Making Money

Hershey School that funds thousands of students every year from around the U.S. Having lost his Irish-American wife Kitty to illness and not having children inspired Hershey to create the Hershey School. These students live in Hershey, Pennsylvania at the school dorms, receiving a first rate education at the expense of the Hershey Trust. In fact, it is this Trust that controls the Hershey company, not the other way around. When he was older and retired, he opened a store on the Atlantic City boardwalk selling Hershey soaps. Hershey had become obsessed with soap manufacturing in his retirement and his soap became a small hit with New York hotels, until one of the patrons of the Waldorf Astoria thought the soap was chocolate and ate it.

Secrets of Making Money

Hershey's life taught me:

1. Success has no monetary figure. Success is about achieving not about earning money. Hershey kept achieving despite his many setbacks and failures and this eventually lead to his success.

2. You must risk all to win all. If you want to win you have to be 100% determined to win with every available resource at your disposable. Hershey invested nearly everything he had in the creation of Hershey, Pennsylvania and was rewarded greatly for his vision.

3. Sales volume is more important than high profit margins. Hershey chocolates consistently

sold because they offered more chocolate in their bars at a lower price than their competitors.

4. Money should be used for greater purposes than self-indulgence. Hershey gave away nearly everything he had before the age of 60. He did this to fund the Hershey School that provided a first class education to thousands from across the U.S.

5. You have to know as much or more than your employees. Hershey was a hands-on leader and spent much of his time experimenting to create new milk chocolate bars and confectionaries.

Secrets of Making Money

WAYS TO MONEY

1. **Become an Employee**

   Advantages: Regular paycheck

   Disadvantages: Can be fired anytime

   Security: Low-Mid

   Cost: None

   Income Type: Active

2. **Start a Business**

   Advantages: High Self-accountability

   Disadvantages: High chance of failure

   Security: Mid-High

   Cost: Mid-High

   Income Type: Active

3. **Buy a Business**

Secrets of Making Money

Advantages: High Self-accountability

Disadvantages: High chance of failure

Security: Mid-High

Cost: Mid-High

Income Type: Active

4. **Marry It**

Advantages:

Disadvantages: Has conditions

Security: High

Cost: n/a

Income Type: Passive

5. **Buy Real Estate**

Advantages: Regular rent income

Disadvantages:

Security: Very High

Cost: Low-High

Secrets of Making Money

Income Type: Passive

Investing In Real Estate

Real estate is the safest and most secure way to become rich, although it may take you 20 to 30 years of your life to achieve it. The point is to start today and that means understanding what the point of investing in real estate is. Real estate is property that is purchased by you for the following purposes:

Renovating & Renting/Selling Them

You have chosen properties to purchase that are fixer-uppers, meaning they are properties that have little to high amounts of cosmetic and/or even structural damage that must be fixed so that you can sell the property for a higher amount than which you bought it. You are essentially bargain hunting and seeking properties that can yield a good profit when sold later. The real gain is witnessed when you renovate and rent properties, holding on to them for 15-25 years in order to sell them at a later time with a higher profit. The longer you are able to hold on to property, the more it will gain in value. The ideal goal should be to just property and to never sell them.

Renovating & Renting Them

You are purchasing properties with the purpose of fixing their cosmetic and/or structural damages in order to rent them out to businesses or individuals. Buying properties and renting them is more important to than selling them. When buying properties to fix them and rent them out, the long term value of the property is additionally more vital than is its short term attractiveness. Commercial properties and industrial properties tend to have longer leases than do residential properties. Also, companies tend to be more careful of the property they are leasing than are residential renters. Obviously it is easier to rent out smaller units and lower priced units so these should be the focus if you are starting with a smaller budget. As you increase your buying power over time, the amount of properties in the high range decreases but your cap rate increases (not always most of the time!).

How Long Should I Hold Property

You should hold property as long as it is generating income for you. Money that is invested in property that is not generating

Secrets of Making Money

income is referred to as "Trapped Capital". It is trapped because your money is in essence trapped without any positive effects for your balance sheet. When the costs of holding that property become more than the Net Profit that is generated for that property, then you should sell it. There are times that you purchase land for the purpose of speculation with the hopes that that property will rise in value over 5 years. This is acceptable because you purchased this land with the specific purpose of holding it a length of time until the value rises. But when you purchase an apartment or flat, either you are going to live in it or you are going to rent it out. That apartment or flat, if vacant, would not serve any purpose for you if it was not be used or rented. Therefore, it is trapped capital. In many situations, it is beneficial to "cash-in" or sell the property at a financial loss in order to "rescue" the Trapped Capital. Nothing feels worse than selling a property at a value that is deemed less than what we feel it is actually worth. But the price that a buyer will pay for the property is what the property is actually worth, not what we think it is worth. So, for example, if I believe a 10,000 square meter piece of land that I own is worth $1,000,000 and a few buyers have offered me approximately $600,000, then my land is worth $600,000. Of course you should hire a professional appraiser to give you an accurate price. But when it comes time to sell, is your appraiser going to buy it? No, the land buyers are the one with the money in their hands so the price set by the appraiser is just ink on a piece of paper. The true value of your property is what buyers are willing to pay for it. After all, they are the ones with the money.

Free the Trapped Capital

By selling off trapped capital, you are freeing up resources (money) to be used for other real estate investments. This money can now be used to invest in real estate properties that are generating income or that have the potential to generate income. The lower your budget, the more picky you should be when selecting a real estate investment. If you are not going to live there, it really doesn't matter where the location of the property is, as long as you have reasonable access to it. In most cases, you will hire a professional property management company to deal with rent collection, maintenance, and associated taxes. For many reasons, individuals possess emotional attachments to real estate. The home in which they grew up, the apartment they fell in love, or the land they were given in inheritance. But the longer you hold on to trapped capital, the more difficult it becomes to detach from it. Although the property value keeps rising during the time that the capital is trapped without generating income, the value that you keep setting for it internally reflects an abstract figure that you hope will materialize in the future. You get the price you want in the future and you may not. But why not use that money to generate income that can result in the purchase of more properties for your real estate portfolio?

Getting Lucky

You will read article after article arguing for luck and

against the belief that luck has
anything to do with business.
Does luck exist and if it does
exist, what role does it play in my
business? You can call it what
you wish, but it is indeed a reality
that some individuals have
access to more resources than
you do. They have access to
more contacts than you do. Luck
has been explained away as
being a consequence of
deliberate steps to prepare
beforehand for the future.
Preparation is indeed a vital
factor in your success but is
preparation alone sufficient to
explain why a business fails and
why it thrives? Luck can be
explained as the right pieces
working in synchronicity to deliver
the desired result. But this would
still not be sufficient to explain
luck for the aforementioned
explanation would still be tied to
preparation. Luck gives you
success when the odds are

Secrets of Making Money

stacked against you. When your chances of winning are low and you still win, that is a clear sign of luck. Your business is affected by luck and no amount of preparation beforehand can guarantee success. Even if you have thoroughly and meticulously prepared beforehand, your chances of winning are still low enough to determine a loss rather than a victory. Therefore it is luck that gives you victory. Can you make your own luck? No. Being in the right place at the right time will create luck. You can underestimate luck as much as you wish but it has played a crucial role in the creation of millionaires and billionaires. They will all tell you that they achieved it by their hard work and hard work is surely a factor in their success. They will omit telling you the most important reason for their success which is luck. People get lucky all the time, just

Secrets of Making Money

ask a Lottery winner that won 200 million dollars. That person randomly chose some numbers and got lucky when their numbers were called. Was that Lottery winner a psychic or did that Lottery winner have someone giving them the winning numbers? No. That person got lucky and that is all that happened. They got lucky and won. There is no formula for winning a Lottery, There is no secret method for picking Lottery numbers. The person just got lucky and won. People get lucky all the time and the lottery winner is a perfect example of a person that has benefitted in real life from luck. If you put yourself in the right place at the right time, you too could get lucky.

Secrets of Making Money

Captain of your Financial Future

We were all born poor but none of us are forced to die poor. You change your future by being pro-active and chasing business. You change your future by being pro-active and making sales on a daily basis. It is up to you to change your financial well being. No one is responsible for your financial well being. You are responsible for your financial well being. If you become poor, your friends may even celebrate your downfall. If you become poor, people that you thought will support will turn their back on you. Everyone wants to be friends with someone who is rich. No one wants to become friends with someone who is poor or that asks you for money. You have to take charge of your financial well being by actively seeking new business opportunities and by

Secrets of Making Money

seeking new customers to sell to.
If you are able to have
consistency and patience, then
you will eventually reach your
goals. You will not win anything in
business by having a negative
attitude. You will not win anything
in business by blaming the world
for your lack of success. You
have to make the decision that
you are going to change your
financial status by seeking
business opportunities. You have
to make the decision that you are
going to change your financial
status by seeking new
customers. No one can do it for
you. You are the Captain of your
Financial Future.

Timing

Opportunities are time
based. If an opportunity is not
seized at the time that it presents
itself, then the opportunity will
pass. This is an important

Secrets of Making Money

understanding that you must
accept in business. Opportunities
pass by and the person that
seizes on the opportunity
receives the benefits from the
risk. Every opportunity is, in one
form or another, a risk. A risk for
winning and a risk for losing.
Without the correct timing, an
opportunity will not appear nor
can an opportunity be exploited.
Business depends on timing. All
of the pieces have to be together
for the opportunity to exist. For
those that create their own
opportunity, they are benefitting
from arranging the time to win. If
you are able to put together the
pieces to create opportunity then
you are also creating the timing
for you to win. In most conditions,
the pieces have to exist and fall
in to place themselves. You
cannot bypass conditions, for if
the proper conditions are not met
to create an opportunity, all one
can do is wait for it. Opportunists

Secrets of Making Money

understanding timing and conditions, which is why they are able to quickly identify when an opportunity presents itself. You cannot force the creation of opportunities. Opportunities can force the creation of Windows Of Opportunity (WOO). By taking advantage of a WOO by investing in it, you are able to reap the benefits of doing so. Imagine if you had bought Amazon stock in 1997. Your investment would have increased many times over the past twenty some years. You would have benefitted by taking advantage of a WOO. On a daily basis, we are presented with opportunities of every kind imaginable. Whether we seize on those opportunities is our choice. In most cases, we choose to do nothing, because doing nothing sometimes feels like the best thing to do. Getty or Hershey didn't build business empires by waiting or by doing nothing. They were always doing something. Inactivity is equal to being non-operational or non-functional. As long as you are moving upwards and forward towards your success, you are winning. A loser is a person that gives up in the face of difficulty. A loser is a person that searches for excuses and for reasons why something will not work. Everyone is clever to an extent and many want to prove how clever they are by attempting to disprove your ideas. Every business idea is an opportunity that can be developed with an org chart, business model, and funding, in to a viable business. Some businesses started with hundreds of millions of dollars and went bankrupt. Some businesses started with nearly nothing and became hugely successful. No one has a crystal ball with the ability to foresee future business events. If fortune tellers were real, then they would be able to predict and change their own futures, would they not? All business is speculation and speculative action. A WOO is a way to profit (or take a loss) by speculating. Money has a value that is dynamic. Money raises or drops in value based on several factors and the Purchasing Power Parity is an effect of that. A WOO allows you speculate by investing in an idea, start-up, or property in order to reap the benefits of its appreciation. Land appreciates and rises in value. Gold, has historically, risen and appreciated in value. Since money has a future value, an investor seeks to hedge themselves against inflation by putting their money in a financial vehicle that will provide them the highest value. Each financial vehicle has an average rate of return on your investment. It is important to try to find the

Secrets of Making Money

investment vehicles with the higher rate of investment. Some would argue that real estate is the best financial vehicle. Some would argue that Gold is the greatest financial vehicle. It is up to you to do as much research as possible to understand the strengths and weaknesses of the various financial vehicles.

 Investing in a business you don't control could result in financial loss.

Money Has Rules

1. Never invest in a business or financial vehicle that you do not directly control. If the ship sinks and in business it often does, you will be angry and you will play the blame game. If the business wins, you will

win. If the business fails, there is a lack of accountability and your investment disappears.

2. Never make an un-collateralized loan. If someone wants to borrow money from you, then they must present some form of collateral that is financially viable. If someone wants to borrow money from you then they should provide something of value that you could sell to recover your money.

3. Gold has been a traditionally safe investment that has risen in value steadily over the past 100 years. There is a reason why all Central Banks of every nation on earth invest their money in Gold bullion. Gold cannot

be reproduced in contrast to paper money which can be printed. Gold is scarce and valuable. The price of Gold is uniform and it is a tradable commodity.

4. Real Estate has been a traditionally safe investment that has risen in value steadily over the past 100 years. Most people that are millionaires became so through the acquisition and sale of real estate.

5. Investing in a business you will start and operate is great and adventurous. Just understand that 90 percent of start up businesses fail in the first year.

6. Money loses value over time which is why money

is invested in financial
vehicles that have higher
and higher rates of return.

7. Friendship and business
   are two different things.
   Don't ruin friendship in
   order to force businesses
   to start.

8. Money is not an end to
   itself. Money is a means to
   provide safety, security,
   and happiness.

9. Money should be never be
   trapped in low producing
   financial vehicles.

10. There is no logic that could
    provide financial
    predictions. All
    investments are
    speculations.

Secrets of Making Money

All investments are a risky and unpredictable venture.

Speculation

All investments are speculation. Nobody can tell you with one hundred percent certainty that a financial vehicle or an investment, will make you a profit. We invest with the hope that we can make a profit. All investments are educated guesses at best and are gambling at worst. On a gambling table, you place your money on something, for example red or black at a roulette table. There is no guarantee of winning but there is a good chance that you will in fact lose your money. Investing in real estate, is not a guarantee, that you will win. It is a speculation. Like all speculations,

Secrets of Making Money

you are optimistic and have hope
that you will succeed by profiting.
In most scenarios, it is difficult to
lose by investing in real estate.
You will be surprised by the
amount of millionaires and
billionaires that have gone
heavily in debt or became
bankrupt through real estate
speculation. Speculation is a form
of gambling. You wish for the
ideal situation to materialize. If it
does you will brag about it to
everyone. If you lose, you will
start to hate the game and will
want to stop playing all together.
The game is not flawed. Your
decisions can, however, be
heavily flawed. The best real
estate investors have an
accountant that tells them
whether it makes to invest in a
certain property. An accountant
consulting you is far better than a
real estate agent consulting you
on profits and losses. The real
estate agent can present you with

46

properties but your accountant will have to tell you if you will profit or lose by investing your money in it. Real estate investments are speculative like gambling, except that real estate has proven itself over the past 100 years, as a relatively safe investment vehicle for slow and steady growth. Real estate investors understand this and seek to take advantage of this "blue chip" safe investment for reaching their goals. Real estate always rises though there are several times in history when real estate has dropped in value. Although there definitely have been times when it dropped in value, real estate has risen steadily in value over the past 100 years. The times when real estate did drop in the United States, are much less than the times that the price of real estate rose. Real estate, can be viewed as the safest and surest way to grow rich over 30 years. If there are people that have gone bankrupt because of real estate, it is because they purchased real estate in a worthless location, they did not have enough of their own capital invested and depended too heavily on loans, and/or were not able to monetize their property. Real estate is the safest form of investment but it is important to have enough capital invested in order to minimize the amount of loan needed (if any). The ideal situation is to purchase a property outright and to not have any open liability. There are several places where property can be purchased for under $100,000. If you are able to spend a large amount of time in research to gain an understanding of real estate prices and the opportunities available, then you will be able to purchase property faster and with greater ease. Even if you do not have the money for a down payment, you can negotiate with an Owner Financed property to absorb the Down Payment in to the Monthly Payments for that buying that property. There are several ways you can do this but it is important to have the mindset of being open to using Creative Financing when purchasing property. Many property owners prefer to not deal with banks or mortgage companies and to transact directly with the buyer of the property. By using creative financing, the range of properties available to you increases.

 Investing in stocks is speculative investing.

Investing In Stocks

The stock market is a particular subject of interest for

investors. Some investors will swear by the ability of the stock markets to make you money. If you had bought Google stock or Amazon stock at their initial public offering (IPO) stages then you surely would have won. But what if they didn't? What if they went bankrupt like grocery start-up WebVan? What if they were destroyed by competitors? There is no guarantee of anything especially winning in the stock market. It is pure speculation. It is a gamble like placing your money on red or black at a roulette table. And like all gambles, you will win some and you will lose some. The only guarantee in gambling is that you will both win and lose. Some people have been very lucky and they have won large amounts on both the roulette table and in the stock market. There are scores of individuals and organizations looking to make a quick buck by selling you

Secrets of Making Money

a formula for making money. There is no formula for making money. We only know what works over the past 100 years. Gold and real estate have proven themselves over the past 100 years. Stocks have a mixed record over the past 100 years. Companies that were number one in the industries 40 years ago do not exist today because those industries don't exist or have changed. Companies that were number one 20 years ago are no longer number one in their industries today. Times change, business models change, technology affects change, and companies transform to survive the business environment. Stocks are speculation like Gold and Real Estate, therefore a wise and prude approach will yield little returns in the stock market. When you buy real estate, the property you are purchasing has a Cap Rate. The Cap Rate is effectively

Secrets of Making Money

your annual Rate of Return on your investment. For example, if a $100,000 apartment has an 8 percent Cap Rate, then it would yield $8,000 per year. Stocks also have a growth rate. The higher the growth rate, the riskier the stock. The riskier the stock, the higher the Rate of Return on your investment. "Blue Chip" stocks like IBM are lauded for their ability to achieve steady growth. The safer the stock the better you will sleep at night, though your sleep may become worrisome since your Rate of Return will become so low. The point of investing in anything is to achieve the highest Rate of Return on your investment. Business 101. Simple business with a simple yet revolutionary formula called "Rate of Return". The Rate of Return is the only thing that matters. Stocks pay Dividends that can be lucrative. The key is finding the companies

Secrets of Making Money

that will pay the highest dividends
and purchasing their stocks. The
troubling part is that their growth
has spikes, the more risky their
stock is. Multi-national companies
that have slow and steady growth
do not experience serious spikes
or dips, but rather climb along a
long slow incline. So stocks are
risky and stocks are speculative,
but they can be hedged against
one another to achieve higher
Rate of Returns. Mutual Funds
are collections of stocks,
purchased in order to yield 15
percent Rate of Returns (in an
ideal scenario). Some self-
claimed clever individuals think
they have created a system, or a
software, or an app, or an
algorithm that can make you
money. If only that were true.
There is no system that can
make anyone money. There are
tips and lessons from others and
experience, but ultimately it
comes down to timing (being in

the right place at the right time)
and luck. Again, there are stocks
that are safe and long term that
will yield a steady Rate of Return.
There are real estate investments
that are safe that will yield steady
growth and a solid Rate of
Return. Gold is safe (if the
Central Banks trust it I will too) as
an investment. But the question
in investing is not always what is
the most safe but rather which
one yields the highest Rate of
Return.

Caroline Otero

Caroline Otero arrived in
Monte Carlo at the age of 19 and
was left virtually penniless. She
put the last of her money on a
gambling table and repeatedly
won, making a fortune and
becoming famous afterwards
because of it. She lived a
fabulous life. The life of the
wealthy where no expense was

spared. She died broke and bitter in a seedy apartment in Paris at age 85. She was famous for breaking the bank at Monte Carlo, which meant that she won all the money the table had. A considerable sum at that time, but Otero increased her wealth and riches through relationships with various rich men. Millions of Francs passed through her hands and she died poor and alone. What happened to her wealth? Spent on lavish goods and on lavish living, without thought of the future. She spent to impress others. Where were those people when she was dying? Nowhere to be found. Live for yourself and your family. Don't live to impress friends. Don't live to impress others. If you want to impress someone, first impress yourself. Show yourself that you have the ability to live beneath your means in order to save with a higher purpose, such as investing in real

Secrets of Making Money

estate or investing in Gold or starting a business or making a meaningful investment. Otero didn't think about her future and so her future was doomed for failure. Life is a long journey filled with miscellaneous expenses and monetary pitfalls. You have to plan for your future by living a quality but frugal. Living beneath your means does not mean that you should live a life without quality. Living beneath your means is about establishing a budget, so that you do not waste money on frivolous activities. Your money should be directed towards generating more money. Money spent on clothes, diamonds, and shoes are wasted. Diamonds wasted? There is no uniform price for a Diamond. Gold prices are uniform, everywhere you go on earth. Diamonds have no set price and pricing diamonds is a difficult speculative task. You could buy a

Secrets of Making Money

$5,000 handbag or $5,000 worth of Gold. $5,000 of Gold will not only not lose value (when averaged over 10 or 20 or 30 or 50 years) but it will more likely than not appreciate. The $5,000 handbag will not be worth $100 in 10 years. Living beneath your means is about directing your money towards investments in valuable items like Gold and Real Estate rather than spending $1,000 on a pair of designer shoes. You are probably asking yourself what real estate you could buy with $1,000. As of this writing, you could buy 1 Acre of Land in Arizona, Nevada, Colorado, Michigan, California, and many other States for $1,000. If you live to impress others, then you are not living to impress yourself. Once you live impress yourself, you will have no need to impress others. You have to have vision about your financial future. If you invest a percentage of your monthly income in Gold and/or Real Estate, you will win when these appreciate. You may not see immediate appreciation. The appreciation may take 5 or 10 or 20 years, but they will rise in value (appreciate). If you fail to plan for your future then you are planning to fail in the future. Live beneath your means and invest in your financial future.

Selling Products

There are many products that you can source and sell online. Obviously the products that sell the fastest online are items that people want the most. You will be surprised however about the products that you didn't know sell well because you never tried to sell them. The easiest way to start selling online immediately is by opening an account on a classified ads

Secrets of Making Money

website like Craigslist. Placing ads is easy and you can test out different format ads to see which ones receive more attention. A person digging in their garage found an antique statue that he sold online for $3,000, allowing to make a down payment on a new car. One person's trash is another person's gold. You will be surprised at how many things you can list in your house or office that you no longer use. You have to be resourceful. Sitting inventory is just as wasteful as trapped capital. Sitting inventory or even un-used items are also Trapped Capital. There is no point in holding on to something that you are not using or that you will not use. The best way to free that Trapped Capital is to sell it. You can take that money, however small it is, and put it in to another financial vehicle. Cleaning out the garage may take on a new meaning. You can

Secrets of Making Money

clean the Garage by selling anything that is not be used. People have been doing it for decades and they call it a Garage Sale. The Garage Sales have moved online in to Classified Ads placed by people trying to clean out their garages by selling off excess stuff. Ebay grew huge off people trying to sell their excess stuff. You can do it too. Not as a business. As a way to free the Trapped Capital and put that in to a higher yielding financial vehicle with a respectable rate of return. The junk in your house, like the junk in your office, are trapped capital just as much as anything else. If it is extra then sell it, if it is junk then get rid of it, and clear out the clutter so you can think clearly. A huge part of the secret of making money is being able to think clearly amid the chaotic business environment surrounding you. By selling off the excess stuff in your life and putting that money in to a better investment, you will be happier and more self-confident about your future financial security. So many times we tend to overlook the resources already in our grasp, already laying around us. By getting rid of the excess stuff we become more focused about what is actually important.

How to Sell

Starting off as a salesperson can be intimidating, anxiety causing, and frightening. The reason why it is so is because we have never been taught properly how to sell. Selling is viewed almost negatively in the public eye. The pushy telemarketer on the phone pitching us something we don't need has been the prevailing image of selling. Salespeople are not looked at as having any special skill. They are viewed as mediocre people that took on a mediocre job. It is an unfortunate view, since selling is rather intricate, complex, and detailed. Before you understand the steps involved in making a sale, you have to understand what selling is. Sales is the process of providing a paid solution to a need. This paid solution may be a service or a good. You, as a salesperson, are helping someone else fulfill their need. You are doing good, because you are helping people receive what they need or want. Each potential customer is known as a Lead. The point of selling is to collect leads so that leads can be transformed in to paying customers. Leads are usually stored in a centralized database software that allows for fast and easy retrieval. As long as you keep filling your Sales Pipeline with Leads, you will have customers. You collect leads for your Sales Pipeline and you follow up with the leads in order to close them (lead them to a sale). In the process of attempting to close them (lead them to a sale), you will discover vital information about your customer (size of the customer, decision-maker's name, etc). By continuously updating the information of your Leads and Customers, you can collect information that will allow you to sell to them with greater ease. The five main stages are selling are important because they allow the sale to happen. The five steps or stages are:

Introduction – In the introduction stage, you are introducing yourself, introducing your company, and introducing your service or product.

Qualification – In the qualification stage you are asking questions that will allow you to understand the needs of the customer. You will also discover the name or names of the decision-makers in that company. You will discover if they are a small, mid-size, or larger buyer. You will discover if there are any conditions that would prevent a sale from happening (no budget, decision-makers are away, etc). If a condition prevents you from making a sale at that time, you must wait until the condition passes for you to move forward.

Sales Presentation – In the sales presentation stage, you will present your services or goods using materials ranging from samples to brochures to pamphlets. The sales presentation should be concise and worded properly to build value in the services or goods you are selling. In the qualification stage, you learned the number of decision makers and their names. There is no point in giving a sales presentation to a person that is not a decision maker. If there is more than one decision-maker, then you must give the sales presentation to all of the decision makers simultaneously.

Handling Objections –
Objections are questions by a potential customer (lead) about your services or goods.
Objections should be received and handled, so that the potential customer (lead) feels comfortable about purchasing from you.
Leads can raise objections about the price and they can raise objections about the quality. If a Lead raises objections about the price, it is because they have not been properly shown the value that your service or good creates. If a Lead raises objections about the quality, it is because they

believe your price is too high. They most likely believe that they can receive a similar quality with a lower price. If you are able to handle their objections properly, then that lead will purchase from you (if a real need exists).

Closing – Closing is the most important stage in the sale process because it is the stage where you ask for their business. There are several ways to close a sale, but the easiest and most straightforward way is to ask for their business. Take out an order form and start writing up their sale. You must believe the sale is going to happen and you must assume the sale. You may have to make a few attempts to close the sale and each attempt may reveal Objections that the decision maker has. The objection, as a buying signal, gives you a window to understand their needs. You must handle the objection in order to move forward again to the closing process of writing up the sales order. A tried and true method of closing is to create a list of reasons why they should buy the service or good versus a list of reasons why they shouldn't. By creating a simple "T" diagram on a blank sheet of paper, with Reasons To Buy on one side, and Reasons Not To Buy on the other side, you can have a visible ad hoc presentation tool that will allow you to close leads.

Whatever method of closing you use, it is important to understand that all the steps are done in to reach the closing stage and close the sale. Everything comes down to closing the sale and getting paid. When you are closing and after you have closed the sale, you must maintain the same character and demeanor as you did have before the sale.

Secrets of Making Money

Professionalism should be the norm.

Starting a Business

Why are some start-ups successful and why do some start-up companies fail? A start-up company seeks to grow to become a "unicorn" or a start-up whose valuation is worth more than $1,000,000,000. Start-ups share similar starts but there trajectory changes due to several factors including business model, future value of target market, leadership style, type, and their solvency. The Internet has featured scores of failed start-ups that featured an unworkable or un-profitable business model.

Secrets of Making Money

Milton Hershey spent most of his time in Research & Development.

Many of the first Internet start-ups had their business plans and related business model scribbled out on a napkin. Venture capitalists were quick to put their funds in to anything Internet related but quickly learned that not all business models are equal. Failed start-ups featured business models that spent more in customer acquisition costs than generated revenue. The Future Value of a Target Market (FVTM) cannot always be calculated. Many start-ups found success in a trial and error manner because the market they were seeking to dominate did not exist. The start-ups were founded to create a product when the "critical mass" of buyers did not exist to justify a venture capital investment.

A "unicorn" is a start-up whose valuation is worth more than $1,000,000,000.

Customer acquisition costs are obligatory especially when the market must be created for the product. The leadership style of the start-up will determine their future success. A disruptive type of start-up can reap great benefits as start-up Uber has experienced. Complimentary types of start-ups are also successful because they act as enablers for that specific industry. Solvency has always been a goal for all start-ups.

Secrets of Making Money

High cash burn rates with little income generation, leads to the downfall of businesses. Start-ups have high cash burn rates causing their venture capital funders anxiety. The faster that a start-up reaches solvency, the sooner the shareholders can be rewarded for their investment. Too many Internet start-ups had to shut down operations because their revenue could not match their intensively high cash burn rate. Spending vital funds on items that do not add value to the customer is not intelligent and burns through a start-up's reserves. By viewing factors such as a start-up's business model, future value of target market, leadership style, type, and their solvency, a venture capitalist will better understand if that start-up is a viable investment.

Secrets of Making Money

Burn Rate

Billionaire Meg Whitman and film producer Jeffrey Katzenberg raised 1.7 Billion Dollars in 2020 and started a video streaming service for mobile phones. They hired 250 people. The service shut down after 6 months. The question is whether it should have started in the first place. Why was this service needed? Quibi, as Katzenberg loved to say, was a me-too business. Instagram Reels already existed. Tik Tok already existed. YouTube. Netflix. Hulu. Why was this service needed? Why did they need 1.7 Billion Dollars? To buy new content? Surely they could have figured out this problem in the initial stages of planning the company. One Billion and seven hundred million dollars is larger than the Gross Domestic Product of many nations on earth. Quibi was a me-too and was not really offering anything that could be deemed innovative or novel.

Outsourcing

One of the secrets of making money is preserving time. When you outsource a task, you are saving yourself time. When you outsource a task, you are conserving resources and saving money. You could try to do everything yourself but you are not a specialist in everything. You would produce low quality work is some things while producing high quality work in other things. You would be inconsistent because it would be impossible for you to try to do everything yourself. If you outsource your tasks or your work, you were able to save your energy for other tasks. Routine and mundane tasks such as graphic design, marketing, and public relations can be outsourced. Many things that you need can be outsourced, saving you money and time that can be spent in better ways. There are some people that like to do everything themselves. They see it as a badge of honor and as a sign of their productivity. If you try to do everything yourself you will end up with mediocre or poor results. One of the first things that you have to do when you start your business is to check your ego. The days of huge overhead expenses and huge offices are done. The virtual company with outsourced services is the norm. Nike is one of the world's largest shoes manufacturers and they do not own a single factory. They outsource the production of their athletic shoes and they outsource many other vital services they use. Outsourcing has, in the past, received a negative image. Companies realized that they had to operate leaner and more

Secrets of Making Money

efficiently while saving money. Outsourcing was the answer and it worked better than they had expected. Car companies moved to Mexico, Tech jobs moved to India, and other industries quickly followed suit. Outsourcing created more value for the end customer because it prevented prices from being raised dramatically on various goods and services. Companies that don't outsource will face stiff competition from their rivals that do.

Trusting People

The only consistent truth when it comes to trusting others is that they will continually let you down. Worse than this is to trust others only to have them betray you over money. As a person that has been stolen from, I can tell you that it is thoroughly painful and heartbreaking to experience.

Secrets of Making Money

Experience is the greatest teacher and the greatest lesson it has taught me is that you cannot trust others to do the right thing. You can trust someone to try to sell a product or sell a project or carry out routine tasks. I am talking about trusting others with money. When it comes to money, people will change very fast and they will always only do what is in their self-interest without taking in to consideration the consequences their actions will have on the lives of others. You could become a business partner of a person that takes out loans and puts you in serious financial debt. You could become a business partner with a person that embezzles the company's fund and encourages pilferage. You could become a business partner with a person that ditches you half way through a project that could potentially net billions of dollars. You could become a

Secrets of Making Money

business partner with a person that uses you as their anger venting board and yells at you constantly. There are various problems that are encountered when it comes to trusting people and money is of course one of them. But there are many more problems that could arise from becoming a business partner with one or two or three individuals. The most famous business persons in history like Hershey and Getty were single persons that were able to become enormously rich using their own mind and labor. Just as there are several bad cases of trusting people, there are several good cases of trusting people. There are many instances where humans have done the right thing, helped others become rich, and helped others reach their goals. That is a personal decision that will be left up to you to make. But for the purpose of protecting

Secrets of Making Money

your financial assets, protecting your income, and protecting your sanity, would it not be wiser to grow safely and slowly on your own?

Starting a Company

There are many considerations to take in to place before deciding which State of the United States or in which nation you wish to incorporate a company. Some States in the US have zero or very low corporate taxes and some nations have very low tax rates that will save your company money in the long run. If you choose to register in the United States, then you will likely want to seek out States like Delaware, Nevada, or Wyoming. If you are registering globally, you will most likely seek out business friendly areas such as Ireland, Hong Kong, or the British Virgin Islands. There are many areas in

Secrets of Making Money

which you can register a
company and legally pay little
taxes. Registering a company
can be done online but it should
be done through a legitimate well
respected services company with
a track record of success. You
can take a Helicopter from Macau
to Hong Kong in 15 minutes,
register a company in 3 hours,
and be back in Macau for Dinner
time. Wherever you decide to
register and start a company, a
few important items have to be
taken in to consideration
including:

1. Yearly Income Tax Rate

2. Registration Fee

3. Ease of Business

4. Labor Pool

5. Annual Fees

Secrets of Making Money

Believe In Yourself

There are a thousand naysayers and haters for every one successful person. Everybody has an opinion or an idea on what is right and what is wrong when it comes to money. The funny thing is that so many persons that give advice have never achieved financial success themselves. If they are so knowledgeable and so well versed in financial matters, then why are they themselves struggling with financial matters? To quote the magician Erdnase "Vanity proves the undoing of many experts". Everyone thinks they know what is best and they make the unseemly error of thinking that they should share their mis-experiences with you. You only need to believe in one person and that is yourself. If you don't know then learn. If you don't know then ask multiple persons for an opinion, but ultimately make the decision for yourself. If you let someone else choose for you, they may or may not have the best intentions in mind for you. If you let someone else choose for you, they may make the wrong decision, causing problems for you without having to bear any consequences for their actions. When you make the decision, you can be confident in your actions even if you make the wrong decision. Business is a trial and error adventure and experience is gained at monetary cost. Although someone may be more specialized in you in one field, that does not mean they are good at business. Business degrees don't make you good at doing business. Business degrees mean you have studied and taken tests. A Business Degree does not mean you have retained that information or that you have any competency in carrying out the various tasks of as business. The only way to learn to do business is by doing business. Reading theoretical knowledge and studying business formulas can help polish your already existing business but they cannot teach you to do business. You should have the confidence to say "No" as often as possible and to only say "Yes" after you have weighed all the advantages and disadvantages of both options. People that interfere in the way you wish to decide financial affairs are seeking to either hurt you or disrupt you. If they are confident that their own ideas are correct then why have they not implemented those ideas in their own lives? If they are so sure of their financial wisdom, then why have they not yet achieved financial success in their own lives?

Secrets of Making Money

Investing in Gold

Nearly 4 billion years ago the earth was bombarded for a long period of time with meteorites. These meteorites left holes in the earth not unlike the craters on the Moon. It is believed that the Moon may have been a piece of a (star) or planet that collided with earth, forming the earth as it currently is, before bouncing off and being trapped in the earth's rotation. The meteorites that crashed in to earth brought rare precious metals with them such as Gold. According to NASA, a 3 meter sized asteroid crashed over the Sierra Nevada mountains (near Sutter's Mill where the 1848 Gold Rush began) weighing approximately 50,000 Kilograms. 50,000 Kilograms of an asteroid could be potentially equivalent to 1,760,000 ounces in precious metals. It was this asteroid that is

Secrets of Making Money

believed to have provided the Gold found at Sutter's Mill sparking the great California Gold Rush. Because the earth's surface was for the most part covered in water, the oceans of the earth contain the largest amount of Gold and precious metals. Gold is precious because it arrived on Earth 4 billion years ago from Space, making it rare and valuable. The world's oceans are said to contain one hundred and fifty thousand tons or more of Gold and possibly even larger amounts of other precious metals. The amount of Gold on earth is limited to the means available to produce it. It is

Gold In Earth's Crust	
Type	Parts Per Million
Sedimentary rocks	.0051
Folded belt region	.0038
Crystalline rocks	0036
Continental crust	.0035

Secrets of Making Money

Oceanic crust	.0035
Earth's crust	.0035
Continental shield region	.0034
Sub oceanic region	.0029
Deep oceanic region	.004

Source: Tung and Chi-Lung

thought that the entire crust and even the core of the earth, contains vast amounts of untapped Gold waiting to be discovered. Gold is an important component in the earth's creation and it is possible that there are molten rivers of Gold far below the earth's crust whose discovery is prevented by our lack of technology. Gold's rarity is because Gold is not a naturally grown commodity like an orange is. Gold was delivered to Earth by space meteorites and it only happened 4 billion years ago. Gold cannot be cloned like plants and even animals can. Gold cannot create more Gold, as the alchemists in the Middle Ages lead potentates to believe. Do you remember the last time you witnessed extended periods of time of space meteorites crashing in to earth delivering you money in the form of precious metals? Neither do I. Gold was sent from Space making it very rare and valuable, unlike fruits and nuts. Saffron may be one of the most expensive spices to purchase but it can be re-planted and re-grown. Gold cannot be reproduced or manufactured from anything but Gold. Looking at the chart by Tung and Chi-Lung, the deep oceanic region contains the least Parts Per Million (PPM) but due to the vastness of the world's oceans comprising the majority of the earth, there may be a lack of testing to determine indeed how much the deep oceanic crust contains. From a geological point of view, it is important to note that

Secrets of Making Money

the entire earth contains Gold. If you are able to take a certain percentage of your monthly earnings and buy Gold, then you will be able to save a large amount of Gold over 5 years. Let us say for example, your monthly income is $4000 per month. If you are able to buy 10 percent of that amount in Gold per month, say $400 per month, then you will have purchased $4800 worth of Gold in one year. Because the price of Gold has historically gone up steadily for the past 100 years, you can count on Gold being more expensive by the second year of your five year gold buying plan. It is important to stick to buy Gold monthly and to save that Gold in a safe and secure location. After 5 years, you will have amassed a considerable amount of Gold and you will (hopefully) see the price of Gold having risen on a steady basis.

Secrets of Making Money

Owner Financing

There are several ways to purchase property and they include:

1. Cash
2. Bank Loan/Mortgage Company Loan
3. Owner Financing

Owner Financing, also known as Seller Financing, is a great option for purchasing property for the first time. There are several websites and apps that you can use to source property that is Owner Financed. The steps involved in purchasing such property are:

1. Finding the properties

2. Contacting the Sellers

Secrets of Making Money

3. Transacting through an Escrow, Real Estate Agent, Real Estate Lawyer.

Owner Financing allows you to save time by bypassing the long and arduous process of acquiring a bank loan. Creative financing allows you to purchase property by having the seller directly finance it for you. There are many real estate investors that started out using creative financing to purchase their first property. It is not embarrassing to use Owner Financing. It is smart business to use creative financing. There is no point in having to pay extra percentage points and fees in order to purchase a property. If a seller will finance it themselves, why not use this option to save time and money? There are many people that are unaware that they can purchase property with little or no money down.

Secrets of Making Money

They have been lead to believe that you have to purchase property the good old fashioned way; walk in to a bank or mortgage company, do paperwork, wait 6 weeks, hope for the best, etc. They have never been shown the easier way to buy property, which is by using owner financing. If the owner or seller is themselves keen on using this method and bypassing banks and mortgage institutions, why would you not use this option? The point of doing business is to lower expenses and maximize profits. Using owner financing allows you to do just that. There are several places that you can begin to start looking for owner financed properties by doing a simple search on Bing or Google or on any search engine you are comfortable with. You have to search for specific keywords to get the proper results.

Secrets of Making Money

Start off by searching by typing the following words in the Search Bar:

1. Seller Financed Properties

2. Owner Financed Properties

3. Seller financing Craigslist

4. Owner Financing Craigslist

5. Owner financing farm

6. Seller financing farm

7. Seller Financing land

8. Owner Financing land

9. Seller Financed building

10. Owner Financed Building

Certain properties perform better under adverse economic conditions such as Truck Stops

Secrets of Making Money

or Industrial Warehouses, because they provide an important need (storage, gasoline depot, etc.) to industries. Certain properties like giant retail stores perform worse under adverse economic conditions. It is important to research the many options available to you and to purchase property that will provide a vital role such as housing or industrial. After visiting a few of the properties, you will have a better understanding of the property type that you are interested in. All property types are not the same. Buying a commercial property has advantages over buying residential real estate because commercial tenants are easier to work with than residential tenants. If a commercial tenant has a problem, they will fix it immediately because the continuation of their business operation depends on it. A

residential tenant will most
certainly require more attention
than a commercial one.

Mining Claims

My Grandfather was an
oilman. My Father was an oilman.
They spent their lives chasing oil
services contracts and partnered
with many major oil services
companies including BJ Hughes.
There are many people that sit
and hope that crude oil will
disappear. 100 years strong. The
world is still dependent on crude
oil and will continue to be
dependent on crude oil for the
next 100 years. There is no such
thing as electric motor 300
person passenger planes. You
may be able to haul 4 people with
electric power, but you will not be
able to fly 300 persons for 12
hours straight on electric power.
Oil is not going anywhere.

Secrets of Making Money

There are over 10 million persons in the United States that receives royalties from crude oil located on their land. By owning the Mineral Rights on their land, they are able to contract with oil exploration companies that pay a small fee to the landowner to explore the land. The fee is usually small, around $500. If the oil exploration company finds oil or gas on the land, they then sign a contract with the landowner to exploit the natural resources on that land. As the landowner owns the Mineral Rights to that land, the landowner receives approximately 20 to 25 percent royalties on the oil produced on the land. All oil wells deplete over time because the oil they are pumping out depletes, but they are usually capped off between 30 to 50 years after the start of exploitation. An oil rig costs anywhere from 5 million to 20 million dollars to purchase. An oil drilling team costs $50,000 per day to operate. The costs are enormous, the oil drilling company pays the costs, and the landowner doesn't have to pay anything at all. The landowner owns the Mineral Rights to the land and can contract with oil and gas companies to explore for oil and gas and to pay royalties in order to exploit the natural resources. The landowner wins big without having to invest anything in order to receive royalties. The landowner did the investing when they purchased land that potentially contained oil and gas on it. Mining claims can also be purchased for Gold placer and Gold lode mining sites. In this scenario, you would purchase the Mineral Rights to a certain land and then you would contract to a mining company on a 50/50 percentage split to exploit the natural resources. The mining company would pay for the operation of the mine and its teams in order to receive the 50 percent royalty. You as the landowner allow the mining company to operate the mine in return for 50 percent of all the Gold (or precious metals) recovered. A 50/50 split is a legitimate offer in a landowner-mining company arrangement. An unpatented mining claim is a mining claim where you only own the Mineral Rights to the land but you do not own the land. A patented mining claim is a mining claim where you own the Mineral Rights and you own the land. Because placer mining is surface mining, an unpatented mining claim is more than sufficient. If the mining claim you wish to purchase or have purchased is perfect for lode mining, then a patented mining claim might be able to allow you to speed up paperwork and permits with the EPA, BLM, or other authorities.

Secrets of Making Money

Power of Compound Interest

There is a secret that many don't talk about but it has fueled investors, businesses, and banks coffers with riches. It is Compound Interest. If you are able to achieve 18 percent return a year on your money through investing in mutual funds, start-ups, miscellaneous financial investments, you will be able to grow your money exponentially over 20 years. 20 years seems like a long time doesn't it? 20 years is a short period of time. 20 years comes and goes like it was 1 year or 5 years. Time doesn't stop for you or anyone. Time keeps moving. Why not let time make you money? If you are able to invest $50,000 in a business that gives you a steady 18 percent a year return on your money, and you are able to put that return back on your original money, then you will earn

Secrets of Making Money

compound interest. $50,000 receiving a steady 18 percent a year with its return put back on your money, will give you over 2 million United States Dollars in 20 years. What? That is right. $50,000 invested in a compound interest account for 20 years will transform in to 2 million US dollars. This is one of the secrets of making money. Using time to win and using compound interest to grow. Every money that is generated is re-invested on top of the principal you had originally invested. This creates momentum. This creates a snowball effect. The power of compound interest is in time and re-investing. As the amount grows larger, so does the return. Compound Interest builds on itself because the money generated annually is re-invested back on top of the principal. If you use this secret of making money, then you will absolutely win and grow. You have to have the discipline to live within your means and to re-invest everything back on top of the principal. If you are able to have the discipline to do this, then you will grow stronger and richer safely over 20 years. Use the power of compound interest to make you money and to make you win. Compound interest, other than real estate and gold, is the safest way to grow steadily rich over time. It will take time. 20 years. It will take discipline. You have to live within your means and you have to re-invest everything that you get back on top of your principal.

Accept Your Flaws

No one is perfect. Everyone has flaws and qualities that they are un-happy about. Just as you would promote your strengths you should also learn to accept your flaws. You should learn to accept other people's flaws as well. If you become so judgmental that everyone around has to be perfect, then you will soon find yourself alone. If you promote an atmosphere that is not flexible to human error, then you will find your employees and independent contractors making every attempt to hide their mistakes rather than to deal with them openly. This will hurt your business financially. You have to be accepting of human error and mistakes in order to deal with the problems they create. You have to accept the flaws inherent in yourself and in your team in order to move past them. Being rigid creates a company culture that is not conducive to change. Your company and your core business may have to change over time and being inflexible will cause your business to fail. Try to be less judgmental about everything and you will find yourself finding new solutions to old problems. As long as you are flexible and open to human error, you can train your team to deal with the errors as they are created.

Reputation of Honesty

It may take 5, 10, or 20 years, but eventually you will be recognized as a trustworthy honest individual if you never cheat and steal from anyone else. Sometimes, scoundrels and villains are celebrated, to the detriment of the earth. In your case, as long as you live a trustworthy life that involves never stealing from anyone else, you will be recognized as a trustworthy individual. This might not mean a whole lot to you. You may ask yourself "Who cares if I am trustworthy"? Many entrepreneurs and important business persons value trust as being among the most important qualities they look for in an individual. In a world of un-trustworthy people, it is very refreshing to meet or re-join with a trustworthy person. Humans have a record, that may or may not be written down, but this record forms their reputation. A person with a trustworthy reputation is invested in and given money to manage. Too many times, un-trustworthy persons have been given important money management roles and they have failed in their duties. A trustworthy person brings a lot to the table. A trustworthy person brings character and fortitude and honesty to the table. That is worth billions of dollars to an entrepreneur. That is worth billions of dollars to a CEO. That is worth billions of dollars to an investor. Money is not the only thing of value in a transaction.

Secrets of Making Money

Reputation is of high value in a financial transaction and a transaction without this reputation can create problems such as theft. A reputation of honesty comes from doing the right thing for many years until you are recognized as a person that possesses a character that is trustworthy. An un-trustworthy individual with a Power of Attorney from you could wreak havoc on your finances and put you in a precarious situation. An un-trustworthy person with a Power of Attorney from you could put you in debt and financial misery for many years. Until you have felt the pain and anguish of transacting business with an un-trustworthy person, you will not be aware of the worth and value of a trustworthy person. A trustworthy person is worth more than money because money can be re-produced but a trustworthy person cannot. They either exist or they don't, but they cannot be printed or re-produced like paper money on a printing machine.

Be Inventive

New money is created when a new source of income generation is created. A new source of income generation is a new source of funding for research and development to create new products. A chess playing machine known as the Turk Automaton was invented by Hungarian nobleman Baron Wolfgang Von Kemplen in 1769. The Turk Automaton was a chess playing machine that was presented to and demonstrated for princes and potentates throughout Europe. The Turk

Secrets of Making Money

The Turk Automaton beat Napoleon in a game of Chess.

Automaton beat the best chess players in the world and even played against Napoleon Bonaparte. Charles Babbage, the father of the modern computer, was inspired to create calculating machines because of it and the modern scientific and literary greats like Edgar Allen Poe wrote about its workings. Poe said "The Turk plays with his left hand. All the movements of the arm are at right angles. In this manner, the hand (which is gloved and bent in a natural way,) being brought directly above the piece to be moved, descends finally upon it, the fingers receiving it, in most cases, without difficulty. Occasionally, however, when the

Secrets of Making Money

piece is not precisely in its proper situation, the Automaton fails in his attempt at seizing it. When this occurs, no second effort is made, but the arm continues its movement in the direction originally intended, precisely as if the piece were in the fingers." When it was demonstrated for the first time, individuals in attendance were in near shock as a machine was able to beat the finest players in the world in Chess. Many theories were created about its workings and much writing was done

Microsoft was founded in 1975.

speculating as to how it operated. Many believed that there was a man hidden inside the machine that allowed the machine to think and move the pieces. If this were

so, the individual would have to
have been a midget so as to be
able to fit in to the machine. But
even if this theory were true,
where would you find a chess
playing midget that was able to
defeat the best chess players in
the world? The other theory was
that it was purely mechanical
movements with the illusion of
intelligence. The machine was
mostly likely pure automata, an
invention that was based around
the movements of gears, wires,
and pulleys. But the creation of a
machine, at that time, was
considered so fantasy-like that
people were in near shock when
witnessing it for the first time. If
even it was purely a machine,
how could a machine defeat the
greatest chess players in Europe
in the late 1700's? What
advanced technologies were
being used that allowed for this?
The Turk Automaton was stored
in a museum that burned down,

destroying the machine forever. Imitations of the machine were created later but the original technology that Von Kemplen created was never seriously analyzed other than through observations of individuals watching the demonstrations. Von Kemplen was an extraordinary and gifted inventor of unusual creations. His Turk Automaton not only created a stir but also advanced the study of automata creation, mostly importantly inspiring Charles Babbage's computing machines. There is an ongoing problem occurring in large and small corporations, whether member run or board run. The problem revolves around a lack of vision in product development. Of course larger companies take longer to make decisions and have to expend much more resources in contrast to smaller companies.

Secrets of Making Money

Lack of vision in product development leads to creation of mediocre products.

But smaller companies will always maintain the advantage of rapidity. Additionally, larger companies, despite vast resources, are not guaranteed by any means to achieve success in a product category that they are not specialized in. Products are developed for today but by the time the product is actually developed and ready for marketing, the product becomes deficient. The mobile phone manufacturing industry has experienced this problem as has the fashion industry. Fads are short term but trends are long term. Although trends are long term, this does not mean that the trend will benefit you, only that the trend will continue to exist. Trends move upward and move downward. Companies develop products to meet the current demand and rarely do companies create products without there being a "critical mass" of buyers available for that market. The company enters the market only to discover their competitors have already launched a better product. What is the solution to creating products that will meet a current or future demand?

 Smaller organizations can make faster decisions.

An intelligent approach to product development would be to identify

Secrets of Making Money

a product category in which their will be a new sub-category created and to create a product now for that future market category. What happens when a me-too product enters a category? Ask Richard Branson and the Virgin Cola brand what happened when he entered the soft drinks category. You can't fight an uphill battle and you won't gain traction by pushing a boulder up a steep hillside. That is where vision steps in and creates an atmosphere of innovation that allows for the creation of a new product that is both useful and fresh. Too many managers are stuck in far off offices with plans and decisions made by committee. The best products in history were created by the vision of a single individual that believed that he or she could make a change. Have vision.

Secrets of Making Money

Don't waste resources on a product that is just a better version of your competitor's.

Investing Green

Whether we like it or not, the earth is getting warmer because of car and airplane pollution. This is a permanent trend that can only be changed if humans alter their behaviors. Besides major advances in solar energy devices and photovoltaic cells (energy storing solar cells), the true dream of solar energy has not yet been realized. Solar technology has been implemented for some devices such as home water heaters or are being used to assist in the generation of energy alongside standard electricity utility service, but have not created an all-encompassing presence in our lives. The use of photovoltaic cells have been centered on providing energy for single family homes. Photovoltaic cells have not yet impacted our lives because the use of photovoltaic cells have not yet been implemented in everyday appliances and devices. Your mobile phone should be solar powered. Your car should be solar powered. Is there any reason your car should be able to drive 200 kilometers per hour? Unless you are a race car driver in a racing contest featuring spectators, you should not be driving speeds that can result in catastrophic accidents.

Secrets of Making Money

By 2050, Solar will be the number one energy source for home energy consumption. Motorcycles emit far more carbon emissions in comparison to automobiles. The use of solar energy to power motorcycles and scooters will greatly reduce carbon emissions in major urban centers that feature populations of over 12,000,000. Solar is self-sustaining and a clean renewable source of energy. Your laptop or tablet computer should be solar powered. In addition, you should have a solar powered scanner and solar powered printer, so that you can always scan and print your files without the need for plugging in to outlets and implementing mechanisms for power conversion. Kitchen appliances should also be solar powered as well because most kitchens have an ample supply of sunlight available to them. Cars, motorcycles, mobile phones, laptops, tablets, scanners, printers, and kitchen appliances should all be solar powered. In addition, portable power packs that store energy should also be solar powered. The use of photovoltaic cells should infiltrate all sectors of manufacturing and its implementation should be a priority rather than an afterthought. Solar energy will change the way we work and the way we operate our companies and investments. The Sun contains enough to power everything on earth. The problem is that humans are not dedicating the time and money to solar. Research and development in solar has been limited.

Secrets of Making Money

Top 10 Reasons Businesses Succeed
(In no particular order)

1. The business met a real need.

2. A demand existed for the service or good.

3. The business was able to sell their goods or services at a lower price.

4. The business had outstanding customer service.

5. The business maintained good relations within the community.

6. The business didn't reduce quality and dramatically raise prices once they achieved a following.

7. The business had employees that went above and beyond the norm in providing service.

8. The business provided services or goods of a higher quality than their competitors.

9. The business advertised heavily.

10. The business created value through providing its goods or services.

Top 10 Reasons Businesses Fail
(In no particular order)

1. Goods or services were of a poor quality.

2. Goods or services were too high priced.

Secrets of Making Money

3. Business was antagonistic towards local community.

4. Business provided poor customer service.

5. Business failed to create and distribute effective advertising.

6. Business didn't create value for customers.

7. Business had poorly trained employees.

8. Lack of demand for the business's goods or services.

9. The business didn't meet a real need.

10. The business raised prices dramatically and/or reduced quality after achieving a following.

Secrets of Making Money

Be Adventurous

Sometimes you have to be spontaneous in business. Some businesspersons have nothing prepared beforehand. They improvise and make ad hoc decisions until they reach their goal. Being adventurous is all about impromptu business decision making. Going in to a situation without preparation purposefully in order to have a flexible and negotiable position. In some situations, such as business negotiations, this is a useful stance to take. A flexible position will benefit you while a rigid position will hurt your competitor.

Be Open Minded

It is impossible to predict with any degree of certainty if you will be successful in one thing or another. You have to be commercially flexible to new business ideas. A business idea without execution is not worth much at all. If you want to attract Angel Investors or Venture Capitalists to invest in your business, then it has to be more than an idea. It has to be a functional business. Even if the business is losing money, it is a functioning business. A business idea is nothing at all. It is an idea that has not been executed. It is an idea that has not been practically tested or applied. Throwing out ideas is for brainstorming in a meeting. Executing the operations of a business are what businesses do and what businesses are about. Sitting and dreaming of an idea would be a waste of your time if you do not implement the necessary steps to make the idea in to a working money generating business. Creating new businesses that align with your core business will allow you to have greater growth. Investing in up and coming start-up companies that will bring a benefit to your core business will allow your core business to grow.

Business Intelligence

The flow of real time business information allows you to make real time decisions. You cannot make decisions for tomorrow based on past information. You have to understand your competitors' strengths and weaknesses. You have to have in-depth knowledge of their products and services. You have to have real time information about their business dealings. Business Intelligence, fuels your marketing and sales department. Your marketing should be in answer to your competitors' advertising. Your salespersons should have in-depth knowledge of your competitors' products and services so that they can sell your products and services better. Business Intelligence is vital to competing with your business opponents. The easiest and fastest way to get information about the seller and their products is to contact them directly, posing as a buyer.

CASE STUDY – AMERICA ONLINE (AOL)

It was the most important thing of my teens. Without it, life was just not as fun. It was really the best for chatting. That is what made me want to be on it and that is probably what attracted everyone to it. It was all about chat rooms and private messaging. It was the greatest thing ever. What started as the Control Video Corporation that featured boxes installed in your house to allow a virtual network, became the world's most famous online network. This was the first major social network and it owes its success to its former CEO Steve Case. Case was a master of building relationships and building private virtual social networks using the AOL model for customers such as Apple. Case spent months living in Palo Alto, California and even convinced the Apple folks to put a desk for him in the Customer Care center. Case, a Political Science degree holder (like myself), used his skills to play the various divisions of Apple against each other. Apple was a highly decentralized company at that time with each division making its own decisions. Case used this to his advantage and was able to convince

Secrets of Making Money

AOL grew so large that it merged with Time-Warner.

the Customer Care department to start a initiative to start a private online network for Apple customers. Case fended off multiple takeovers from eccentric Steve Wozniack (who had amassed up to 20% of AOL stock at one time) but Case slipped in a "poison pill" clause in the Bylaws through the Board of Directors, that would make buying AOL prohibitively expensive for a company attempting a hostile takeover. Case kept immensely strenuous hours at AOL and he always compared keeping AOL alive to "maintaining a space shuttle indefinitely in space." Case spent most of his hours as the de-facto Mayor of AOL and spent much of his time exchanging emails and chatting online with customers. Case shined most during AOL's internet war with Microsoft that sought to decide who controlled the Internet Service Provider business in America. Case's input made AOL user friendly and hip, in comparison to Compuserve (a dinosaur) and Prodigy (too bookish). Case's only mistake came when he lead the takeover of Time Inc, one of the largest media corporations on earth.

 Data gives you the information you need to make decisions.

Information Driven

One of the secrets of making money is having information. Information drives your investments and information provides you with new and more viable opportunities. Reading the newspaper takes on a whole new meaning when you view it from the lens of a speculative investor. You are looking for indicators that could create changes in prices. A looming war in a 3rd world country could easily affect the prices of Gold and Crude Oil. A deal like Brexit does send shockwaves through financial markets and cause certain commodities like Gold to rise. A new nation joining the Euro zone could cause the prices of the real estate in that nation to rise. When you look at a newspaper through the lens of a speculative investor, you begin to notice new things. You begin to notice events and you will start to ask yourself how these events affect financial markets. Reading news about an oil glut and oil dumping could give you clues as to the direction that oil prices will go towards. You have to keep abreast of the latest news in order to understand what events are occurring. Once you understand the events occurring, you can begin to try to speculate as to how the financial markets and certain commodities will behave. Whether you are Bullish or Bearish regarding financial markets, you have to stay aware of the next event that will take place. Once you have analyzed the event and the players involved, you can begin to try to draw conclusions as to how the players in this event will act. Information is the lifeline of speculative investors. Without constant flow of information, speculative investors will be hard pressed to make a decision, if any. This is why companies pay thousands of dollars per year for software that feeds them information. This information allows them to stay informed as well as be able to make informed decisions regarding financial matters. Speculative investing is information driven and will continue to be as long as events affect financial markets. Some would argue that money "makes the world go around" but a truer statement would be that "information makes the money that makes the world go around". Information is expensive and time consuming to gather. Consultants are hired by speculative investors specifically because they have the information already available. Consultants can tell you the price of Cocoa on an actual farm in the Ivory Coast while the news channels and news sources can only tell you the price of Cocoa on global financial markets. A professional paid consultant has spent years gathering information that they "rent" to speculative investors and companies. It would be too cost intensive and time intensive to gather this information yourself, but by hiring a professional consultant you can save the time and money you would have wasted trying to re-create what they have already achieved. Information is part of the winning formula for a business and without a steady flow of it, there is difficulty in top level decision-making. Decision-making is based on available and new information. Consultants have amassed "best practices" that allow them to offer you information not available to the public.

Woes of Inflation

Inflation is an unfortunate reality. The price of everything, from houses to land to Gold, rise over time. Inflation is caused when the supply of money is increased by the Government in order to pay off debt. If you look at a chart of inflation over the past 100 years, you will notice a pattern. Inflation has been a constant reality over the past 100 years and will continue to be an issue as long as Governments print money to pay off their debt. A 5 bedroom house in Los Angeles would have cost approximately $50,000 in the early 1970's. That same house is nearly $1,000,000. The price of Gold was $36 an ounce 50 years ago. How much is it today? As of this writing, it is nearly $2,000 an ounce. You can see that inflation results in the prices of commodities and goods rising because the cost of production and the cost of labor has increased over time to keep up with the rate of inflation. In order to keep up with inflation, you have to increase your income over time. The higher the rate of return the more assured you are that you will beat inflation over time. Some financial vehicles such as Gold or Real Estate have done well in beating inflation. Some financial vehicles such as Stocks have had mixed records (some wins and some losses) against inflation. Whatever financial vehicle or vehicles you choose to beat inflation, you must realize that inflation is a constant variable that must be taken in to consideration when choosing which financial vehicle to invest in. All financial vehicles are not equal and some have a better ability to fight off inflation. Inflationary techniques used to boost economies such as Quantitative Easing are controversial because their effects are not always visible. Inflation hurts economies because it creates instability in markets.

Secrets of Making Money

Compound Interest grows your money exponentially.

Money Makes Money

It is a cliché but a well understood one that investors live by. Your money is invested in order to make you more money. Why is it important to make more money? Because of Inflation. Inflation causes the price of everything to rise. Your $50,000 in 20 years will be worth less than it is today because the prices of goods and services will go up. The prices of goods and services rising is an unavoidable reality that must be comes to grips with and plans must be made to avoid becoming poorer because of it. If you understand that inflation is an economic reality, then you can find financial vehicles that are able to beat inflation, like Gold or Real Estate. Cars, depreciate over time. Even the building structure on land may depreciate, but real estate will appreciate over time. The jewelry display cases which cost thousands of dollars will depreciate, but the Gold held within them will appreciate. The price of food rises because of inflation just as the price of all material goods rise because of inflation. Services, face the same fate as goods. A price of a good or service is not dictated by supply and demand but rather it is set by the cost that it takes to create a good or provide a service. Even if no consumer wants Gold, Central Banks will still purchase Gold and use it as a commodity. Even if no one buys real estate this year, people will still need a place to sleep and a place to work from in the future. Real Estate will always carry a demand because of its functional use. Gold, has uses ranging from military to medicine, which is why it is a sought after precious metal. The price of both Gold as well as Real Estate will continue rising to meet or beat inflation, which is why both Gold and Real Estate are viewed as relatively safe investments with a very low risk factor. Anyone that claims to hold some secret formula to making money is probably trying to con you or cheat you. You can only do what works for you. We can only look at what has traditionally and historically worked for others. Since we know that over the past 100 years, both Gold and Real Estate have risen to meet or beat inflation, we can say with certainty that both Gold and Real Estate are tried and tested methods for safely investing. This doesn't mean that people haven't lost money on Gold and/or on

Secrets of Making Money

Real Estate, because there have been scores of millionaires that have lost everything trying to take wild risks. It is an obvious fact that the more you invest in a deal that goes as planned, the more you will gain. Also it is important to add that the less you invest in a deal goes as planned, the less you will gain. It is up to you to be able to gauge your own level of comfort when it comes to investing. Some people are more comfortable with smaller deals and smaller profits that time less time to execute. Some people are just concerned with bigger deals and bigger profits that take a longer time to execute. As long as you understand you are fighting inflation by attempting to increase your rate of profits, you can win. You have to beat inflation by increasing your investments in order to create additional revenue in order to be able to combat inflation. Your

Secrets of Making Money

investments have to grow faster than inflation. If inflation is 3 percent annually then you have to invest in, for example, real estate that will give you 8 percent return on your investment. As long as your appreciating investment's rate of return is higher than the rate of inflation, you are ahead and winning. Every year, you can grow your investment fund by re-investing profits back in to the fund. The larger the fund grows the more opportunities become available to you that will have the capability of reaping greater profits. Money makes more money because re-investing profits back in to the fund creates a snowball effect and provides you with the momentum to invest in larger projects. If you take the time to analyze an investment properly used a talented accountant, the chances that you will lose on an investment becomes slimmer.

Secrets of Making Money

Many people have lost money trying to re-invent the wheel in order to create "unicorns" or billion dollar companies. The key is starting small and growing your investments. Everyone wants to "shoot for the Moon" without wanting to "start from the ground". The journey of a 1000 miles does start with a single step. The key is to believe in yourself, believe in your experience and knowledge, and believe in your will to succeed. Obviously, not all investment opportunities are created equally and some will have higher rates of return than others. It is important to understand, that the higher the rate of return in an investment, the more risk involved. This is not always true, but it is mostly true in investing. Higher rates of return mean higher risk. Some people are completely comfortable with riskier investments and some people will not be able to sleep at night had they invested in a risky investment. A Mutual Fund is a safer investment than a stock because it spreads out the risk and reward between the various stocks in the Mutual Fund portfolio. A piece of land is a safer investment because it is known that land will appreciate and rise in value, according to charts detailing the past 100 years of real estate prices. Acting as an Angel Investor in a start-up tech company is a riskier investment because there is no guarantee of this company or their service succeeding in capturing market share in their industry. The tech company could become bankrupt and the money of the Angel Investor is gone permanently without any reward to compensate for risking the investment. If the start-up tech company is purchased by a larger tech company, the reward is much higher than the reward for investing in a safer investment like Real Estate. The greater the risk, the greater the reward. The younger you are the more risks you should take. The older you get the less risks you should take. The older you get, the less you are able to accept risk without permanent damage.

 Liabilities reduce your cash flow.

Golden Rule

Buy Assets and avoid liabilities. Liabilities destroy your cash flow and prevent you from raising the funds necessary to invest in more assets. You may have much assets but if you had to stack up liabilities, then these liabilities reduce your capital.

Secrets of Making Money

Un-happy
people
spread
negativity.

Dealing With Ghosting

Whenever people hear that you are starting a new business, this may make them jealous. In order to make themselves feel powerful, they may try to avoid you on purpose. It is called Ghosting, for some odd reason. You have to believe in yourself and believe in your business ideas. You have to have the self-confidence to forge ahead in the face of naysayers and jealous individuals. If they are treating you in a way that makes you feel alone and isolated, it is because they do not want you to succeed. It is alright to be confronted with individuals of such nature. They love to give you advice yet how many of them have been successful in their business careers? How many of them have been successful in entrepreneurship and commerce? As long as you believe in what you are doing and you trust your abilities, you will be successful. You can surely take advice from anyone and you should take advice from specialists, but unless these people judging have themselves been successful, why should you listen to them? Business is a process of making mistakes. Experience is gained at great cost and in risk. If you have lost in business then you have been successful because you tried, which is more than could be said about some of the people giving you advice. You should trust your own instincts in business but utilize the experiences of others as the parameter for success or failure. Everyone thinks they can do everything better than everyone else. Theories and debate are great for after dinner conversation. In business, experience is the greatest skill that is acquired through time and diligent effort. A person that has lost millions of dollars has gained millions of dollar of experience. The former CEO of IBM, Thomas Watson, was originally a cash register salesperson. Only by going through the experiences can you amass valuable experience. Business experience is gained over time and it could take many years to be realized. Business takes many parts working together in synchronicity to achieve success. If you are afraid of losing money to make money then you will not be a good businessperson. Business if first and foremost about taking risk. Many people are unable to exercise the patience needed to undergo risk. You have to understand that Business is nothing but risk. It is a risk for reward, and the greater your risk the more you will gain if you are successful.. It is impossible to do business in a state of nervousness. Business has to be conducted in a patient and calm nature. As long as you are sure of your abilities and you have calculated your risk, then you can manage your risk level and have some degree of understanding as to how the project or investment will play out. Anxiety is, more often than not, caused by over-thinking and a wild imagination. Nervousness can lead to excess cautious behavior which means that even if you win, the win will be small because you were afraid to take the necessary risks to win. You can't do business in a scared manner. You should always be cautious but if cautiousness leads to hesitancy, then that is counterproductive. If you have done all the calculations necessary to have understanding of what could go wrong, you will be able to conduct business with greater confidence.

Secrets of Marketing

What is marketing? Marketing is business communication created with the purpose of generating demand for a product or service. Everyone understands that they have to create social media pages and post on them. Everyone understands what a press release and how it is used. What few understand is the process involved in generating demand. In order to generate demand, your product or service has to either be of a higher quality than your competitors or your product or service have to be lower priced. You have to differentiate and create a difference in the category you are competing in. You won't be able to win with a me-too product that is not significantly lower priced or of higher quality than your competitor. No two products or services are created equally and no two marketing campaigns are similar. Every situation requires its own unique solution for winning. Certain audiences require specialized messages geared just towards them. In marketing, you have to understand the demographics and social interactions of your target audience. Once you understand this, you can test out several messages and gauge the level of interest generated from each ad. Marketing campaigns are time and cash intensive. A media buyer purchases x amount of advertising space from several media outlets and ad agencies. Graphic designers are paid to design the advertisements and copywriters are paid to create the text of the ad. The most important part of the entire process is the ad copy (text) created by the copywriter. Each product or service has a quality that can be attributed to it. For example, xyz product has the *fastest* delivery or abc company has the *friendliest* customer service. The ad copy uses several methods (play to logic, play to emotion, etc) to entice potential customers to seek out that product or service. What is being communicated sets the tone for the brand and helps build an image of trust in the mind of the consumer. Building trust in a brand can only come out when a customer has purchased a product or service from that brand. Brands are contracts of trust between a buyer and a seller. Brands are an assurance to the customer that you are a quality product or service. This is why brands take so long to build. It takes time to build trust in a brand, sometimes 20 or 30 years or more. Brands are a mark of trust. A sign that you can be trusted to purchase from. A sign that you will not rip off the customer and that you will do what you say you do. People don't fall in love with products. People fall in love with brands. There isn't any prestige in purchasing generic goods or services. Certain commodities like Rice may be purchased in bulk but once it is packaged like Uncle Ben's Rice, it becomes a brand. People will pay a premium price for a brand name product or service because of the perception that a brand is more valuable. Some brands take on a separate value of their own because of their ability to generate revenue just from their name and logo. Licensing and merchandising arrangements are standard practice for brands like Disney. Brands that take on too many un-related products or services risk diluting their brand name and reducing public trust in their brand. A brand that takes on too many products or services that are un-related to the core business risk making their brand name mean several things simultaneously. In the mind of the consumer, the brand is the product or service. In the mind of the business owner, the brand is an extension of the product or service. This is an incorrect understanding. The correct understanding is that the brand is the product or service. The consumer is not drinking a carbonated soda, in the mind of the consumer they are drinking American values, which is what Coca-Cola represents. The consumer is drinking the brand and that brand represents certain values that make drinking Coca-

Secrets of Making Money

Cola appealing to the consumer. You have to understand what values your brand stands for and to represent those values in your brand's marketing and advertising copy. For example, let's say you were starting a Outdoor Clothing brand geared towards young campers. You would want your brand values to be:

Rugged

Fresh

Innovative

Now you have chosen your brand values; Rugged, Fresh, Innovative.

All your marketing and advertising copy and imagery for the fictional Outdoor Clothing brand would attempt to present a rugged, fresh, and innovative message. The perception of your brand is shaped in the mind of the consumer by the values of your brand. The values of your brand is what potential customers will identify with and attract them to your product or service. Customers are attracted by your brand's values and they develop a relationship with your brand through your core values. For example, in the case of the fictional Outdoor Clothing company, their core values are rugged, fresh, and innovative. Their target audience is young campers. Young campers will fall in love with their core values and develop a relationship of trust with the brand. This trust will create repeat business and referrals for new business. It is much easier and much more cost effective to get repeat business and to get referrals for new business than it is to acquire new customers through advertising.

Secrets of Making Money

Customer Acquisition costs are what it costs you to get one new customer. In the case of some companies, their customer acquisition far exceed their revenues, which results in bankruptcy. Acquiring new customers is difficult and cost intensive which is why many companies focus their efforts on repeat business and acquiring new business through referrals. Once a customer has purchased a product or service, constant communication with that consumer will make that customer in to a lifelong loyal customer. Companies, such as mobile phone service providers, assign a Lifetime Value to customers because they understand that once that customer has purchased their product or service, the switching costs will be too high for that consumer to buy from their competitor. Business is about generating trust and building long lasting relationships. These relationships are worth money and they can help you grow financially stronger. Companies with poor customer service develop bad relationships with customers and this results in them losing customers. Many of those lost customers will tell other potential customers about your lack of service or sub-standard product. You gain new business when your brand fulfills the trust that it has promised and you lose new business when your brand fails to honor the promise it has made to consumers. Business is about honoring commitments with consistency so that trust is developed over time. When businesses fail to honor their commitments, they will not only lose new business but they will also lose the current customers that they have spent money acquiring. If a company loses 8 percent of its customers per month, then it will have lost nearly 100 percent of its customers in one year. A business has to keep generating new customers in order to remain solvent. The process of generating new customers is least expensive when done through referrals and repeat business. The process of generating new customers can be prohibitively expensive if advertising is the only option that is available. There are many examples of brands using viral marketing to generate word-of-mouth advertising. Earned media or free publicity, is another method used by brands to generate attention and interest in their products or services. Whichever method is used, you have to understand that you are not selling products or services. You are selling values and those values are what attract the consumer to purchase. Marketing is about generating demand for what you will offer or are offering. Marketing makes the brand name known so that sales become effortless and automatic. Viral marketing has been used effectively by individuals such as Richard Branson. Steve Jobs of Apple was famous for his ability to hype a product and generate buzz. Things like jumping out of an airplane, running down the street in a Wedding Gown, bringing an elephant to a trade show, and other Public Relations stunts have been used by various companies to generate "buzz" or word-of-mouth. It is known as viral marketing and companies have generated earned media by doing it. Earned media is free publicity and it is worth several times traditional advertising.

Secrets of Making Money

Have No Fear

What's the worst that could happen if you approach an angel investor or venture capital company? They say no. Are you going to give up? Or are you going to keep pushing forward until you find the right investor? It may take time and effort, but it can be done. Many have walked this path before. What one person can do, another person can do just as good or better. You cannot have fear of rejection. You should think of those as having rejected you as people that just missed out on a golden opportunity. It is their loss, not yours. You will keep moving forward in the face of difficulty because you are a winner. You have to have no fear in business. In business you have to have courage and you have to have patience. All great things take time to come together. Rome wasn't built in a day. You have to have confidence in your business so that you are able to walk and talk fearlessly among angel investors and venture capitalists. The only people that should be afraid are the ones that fail to invest in your business opportunity. They should be afraid of losing out on potentially millions or billions of dollars. They should be afraid of missing out on investing in your business opportunity. You should be confident of your skills, education, abilities, and business operations, so that you can confidently present your business plan and answer the questions of potential investors. What is the worst that could happen to you? They decide to not invest in your business opportunity. What happens after that? You move on to new angel investors and venture capitalists. You do not get stuck in a state of stagnation.

Secrets of Making Money

You keep moving forward and fight the right interested investors that can bring benefit to your business opportunity. You should never be afraid of doing good for others. When you offer an investor the ability to make higher rates of return, you should be applauded and awarded for doing good for others. You are helping someone achieve financial success. That is a good deed and one that is worth of honor. This is why you should have no fear or be intimidated when speaking with potential investors in your business opportunity. You are helping them. They should be thanking you and telling you how much they are grateful. If you help someone achieve greater rates of return on their money, they should be grateful for helping them achieve their financial goals. Have no fear when speaking with investors.

Secrets of Making Money

Angel Investors

Angel Investors are individuals with a high net worth that have a track record of making small investments in start-up companies. Angel investors win big if the company is sold and lose small if the company goes belly up. Because the investments that angel investors make are in start-up companies, there is a greater reward, should that company become successful. Angel investors are easier to communicate with and more approachable than venture capital companies. Angel investors are not associated with venture capital companies and that makes them easier to do business with. The process of Presentation to Investment occurs faster, which is a huge benefit to a cash strapped start-up company.

Secrets of Making Money

Venture Capital

Venture Capital investments can help your business grow. You don't need to always find a venture capital company to invest in your business as you can also seek out Angel Investors. Angel Investors are individuals with a high net worth that seek out start-ups to invest in. Whether you seek out Angel Investors or Venture Capitalists or Venture Capital companies, you have to understand the role of money in your business. The person or company that takes the risk of investing in a new and novel business will win greater when the business becomes successful. When you talk about Apple, people get nervous when talking about how the company started and how the original shares of that company were divided. Surely the people that

Secrets of Making Money

put in the work like Steve Jobs deserve the most shares, do they not? No. No they don't. The person that was wild enough and visionary enough to invest in the start-up stage of Apple deserves the most shares. The person that invested in Google or Amazon or Facebook in their early start-up stages deserve(s) the most shares. All business ideas are a risk and there is no way of knowing with any certainty if a business will become successful in the future. Venture Capitalists are the ones that take the greatest risk in any start-up company. Facebook would still be in a garage or dorm room somewhere if Peter Thiel and Eduardo Saverin didn't invest in it. There is no instance of any business having become successful without money. The money has to come from somewhere. The money won't come from wishing for it. You

Secrets of Making Money

either have to have your own
money to invest in it or you have
to get an investor (Venture
Capitalist or Angel Investor) to
invest in it. Business ideas are
just ideas. Saverin and Thiel
didn't invest in an idea. They
invested in a start-up with
barebones infrastructure and
barebones development, but
there was something there. If you
approach venture capitalists and
angel investors with an idea they
will tell you that an idea is not
worth much at all. An idea is a
rough un-developed concept
without the implementation. The
implemented idea is worth
money, not the idea itself. You
cannot patent or license an idea.
Ideas, unto themselves, are
worth very little. Ideas don't
generate revenue, businesses
do. Every business was at one
time an idea that was
implemented and executed. Once
the idea has been implemented,

then you can present that
implementation to an Angel
Investor or Venture Capitalist.
Everyone thinks the glory lies in
being the face of a start-up and
some start-ups have certainly
generated more hype than
others. The reality is that the
glory lies in being the wallet of
the start-up. Once that start-up
takes off, then you will stand to
greatly benefit from that risk. No
two risks are alive and each risk
carries its own benefits and
awards just as each risk carries
its own shame and losses. There
have been Angel Investors that
have put a quarter of a million
dollars in a business and lost
their money when the start-up
business failed to take off. There
have been Venture Capitalists
that received five percent
commission for raising funds for a
business start-up and received
an even greater return when the
start-up business was sold to a

Secrets of Making Money

big tech company. The point of Venture Capitalists is the same as yours, to receive the highest rate of return on your investment. Venture Capitalists and Angel Investors take calculated risks with the hope of receiving higher rates of return from putting their funds in a risky or riskier investment vehicle. Although Venture Capitalists are open to taking on riskier investments, they will most certainly demand large percentage of shares for their investments. Angel Investors invest less money than a Venture Capitalist but Angel Investors also take less percentage in that start-up business. Venture Capitalists sometimes refer to themselves as Sharks and that is because they are always hunting for new investments. They are open to receiving new business but that start-up business has to be economically viable. In other

words, there has to be a real
reason to invest in that business.
There has to be a reason that
start-up should or shouldn't exist.
Because Venture Capitalists and
Angel Investors commit their time
to studying various investments,
they have a better understanding
of the business models that will
become successful and of the
business models that will fail. You
need money to fuel your business
start-up and doing it with money
other than your own can be
refreshing. You may not always
be able to fuel your business
start-up with your own money.
You may have to rely on other
people's money in order to take
your business from start-up to
seasoned successful business.
Many venture capitalists or angel
investors will refuse to invest in a
start-up business in which you
don't have your own money
invested. It is referred to as "Skin
in the game". The investor's logic

Secrets of Making Money

is that if you believe so deeply that this business will be successful, then you should have invested your own money in to the business. Venture Capitalists or Angel Investors will become suspicious about a start-up business whose founder has not personally invested their own funds in the business. If you haven't invested your own funds, then it is a sign that you may not believe that your business is worth investing in. If you are the founder of the start-up, you have most likely invested time and money in your start-up. You have to be excited and in love with your business so that others will feel the same about it. You have to be the frontrunner in pushing your business to greater success. Before you meet with the angel investors or venture capitalists, take time to study your business plan in-depth and write down a list of questions that you think they might ask you. They will ask you questions to find out how much you have invested and they will ask you specific business questions about your business operations. They want to know what you know and they want to figure out where you have failed. Angel investors and venture capitalists work for money, are greedy, and don't want to be left behind from investing in the next billion dollar business. They are cautious however and they will ask you some questions to find out how well versed you are in your own creation. If you are unable to answer simple questions, that is troubling to investors and a sign that you are either not forthright and honest or that you are evading answering or that you really don't know about your own business. Either way, they will view this as a negative. If you want to be successful you have to be

prepared beforehand to answer
as many questions as they may
have.

What You Need:

Executive Summary – Short
summary that briefly explains
your business.

Business Plan - Well written, well
researched Business Plan will
help you to convince the Venture
Capitalists and/or Angel Investors
of the value and viability of your
start-up business.

Meeting Presentation – It is vital
to meet with the Venture
Capitalists or Angel Investors in
order to receive a definitive
answer. In the meeting
presentation, you want to give a
clear presentation and answer
any questions the investors have.

Secrets of Making Money

Conclusion

Business is a world unto itself and it is a dynamic one. Business in 50 years now will look different than it does today but the business principles that you will use today are just as applicable tomorrow. The more you do business, the better you will get at it. Nothing can replace experience, for experience is and will always be the greatest teacher. All business is risk and all business is speculation. As long as you have the courage to bear the difficulties involved in business you will eventually become successful. Have a clear mind and a positive attitude. Understand that all great things take time to mature and to reach their peak. Have patience and maintain focus in the face of your difficulties. Do not let setbacks dictate your future actions. Do not let setbacks create bitterness. Everyone fails. Everyone also wins. Whether you fail or you win, you should stay humble and focused on your financial future.

Secrets of Making Money

MIKAZUKI PUBLISHING HOUSE™

(U.S.P.T.O. Serial Number 85705702)

1. 25 Principles of Martial Arts
2. 25 Principles of Strategy
3. American Antifa
4. American Bookstore Directory
5. Arctic Black Gold
6. Art of War
7. Back to Gold
8. Basketball Team Play Design Book
9. Bernie Sanders Revolution
10. Boxing Coloring Book
11. California's Next Century 2.0
12. Camping Survival Handbook
13. Captain Bligh's Voyage
14. Coming to America Handbook
15. Customer Sales Organizer
16. DIY Comic Book
17. DIY Comic Book Part II
18. Economic Collapse Survival Manual
19. Farrakhan Speaks
20. Fashion Design Shoes Coloring Book
21. Fidel Castro Speaks
22. Find The Ideal Husband
23. Football Play Design Book
24. Freakshow Los Angeles
25. Game Creation Manual

Secrets of Making Money

Secrets of Making Money

Facebook.com/MikazukiPublishingHouse